Life After Graduation

It's What You Learn After You Know It All That Really Matters

An Inspirational collection of wit, wisdom,
scripture and common sense.

It's a "quick read" that really delivers a short but
powerful message on friendship, life, money, God, love,
faith, family and other basics for living.

Now that you have finished school,
it's time to start your education!

Brownlow

ISBN 1-57051-405-4

9 781570 514050

UPC

7 03800 14054 8

You might as well like yourself. Look how much time you're going to have to spend with you.

Jerry Lewis
(the Nutty Professor)

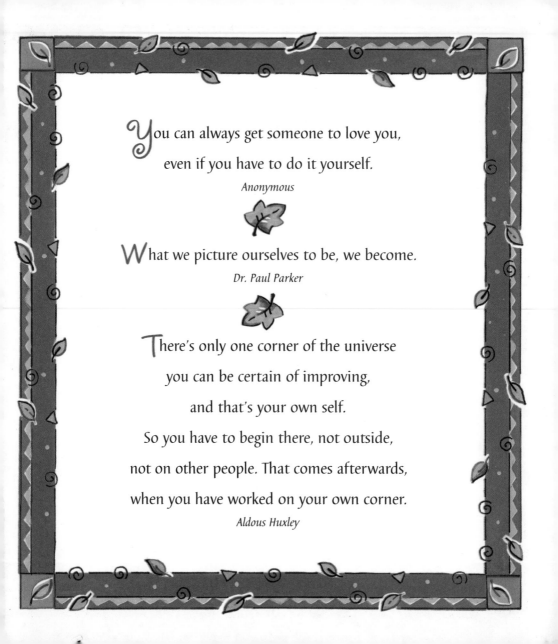

You can always get someone to love you,

even if you have to do it yourself.

Anonymous

What we picture ourselves to be, we become.

Dr. Paul Parker

There's only one corner of the universe

you can be certain of improving,

and that's your own self.

So you have to begin there, not outside,

not on other people. That comes afterwards,

when you have worked on your own corner.

Aldous Huxley

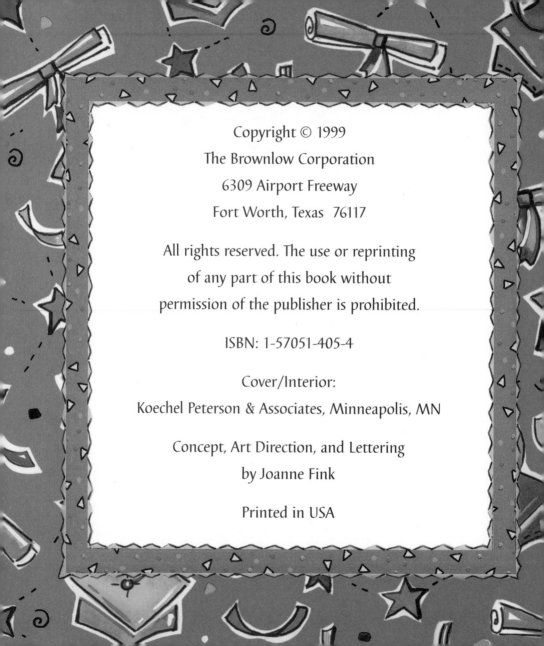

ISBN: 1-57051-405-4

Cover/Interior:
Koechel Peterson & Associates, Minneapolis, MN

Concept, Art Direction, and Lettering
by Joanne Fink

Printed in USA

A Special Gift

For

April

With Love From

Y & G

Date

Spring, 2003

Table of Contents

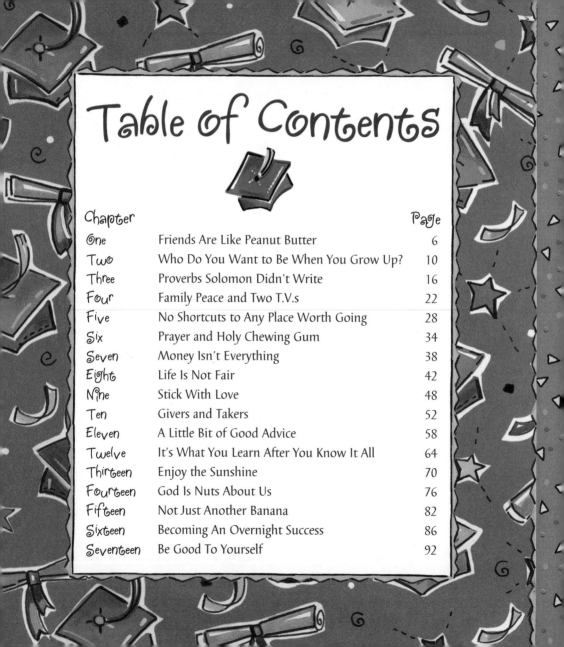

Life After Graduation

Compiled and Written by
Paul C. Brownlow

Illustrated by
Allison Jerry

Brownlow

CHAPTER ONE

Friends Are Like Peanut Butter

Friends are like Peanut Butter.

They come in two varieties—Regular and Extra Crunchy.

Try to stock up on both kinds.

Regular friends are good everyday.

But the Extra Crunchy friends add

that special burst of flavor to everything.

Paul C. Brownlow

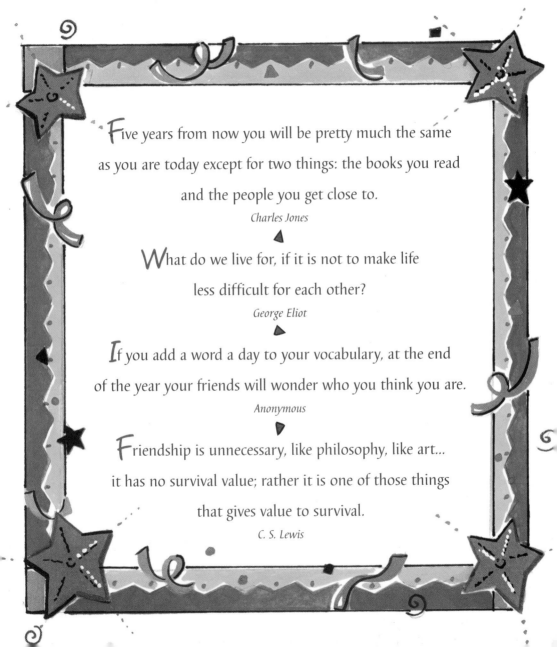

Five years from now you will be pretty much the same
as you are today except for two things: the books you read
and the people you get close to.

Charles Jones

What do we live for, if it is not to make life
less difficult for each other?

George Eliot

If you add a word a day to your vocabulary, at the end
of the year your friends will wonder who you think you are.

Anonymous

Friendship is unnecessary, like philosophy, like art...
it has no survival value; rather it is one of those things
that gives value to survival.

C. S. Lewis

Anyone with
a heart full of
friendship has
a hard time
finding enemies.

Anonymous

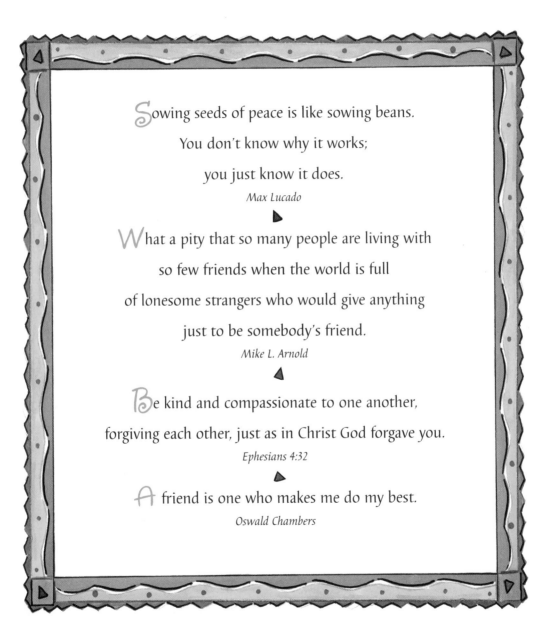

Sowing seeds of peace is like sowing beans.

You don't know why it works;

you just know it does.

Max Lucado

What a pity that so many people are living with

so few friends when the world is full

of lonesome strangers who would give anything

just to be somebody's friend.

Mike L. Arnold

Be kind and compassionate to one another,

forgiving each other, just as in Christ God forgave you.

Ephesians 4:32

A friend is one who makes me do my best.

Oswald Chambers

CHAPTER TWO

Who Do You Want to Be When You Grow Up?

Growing up means choosing to meet
someone else's need rather than your own.

Anonymous

More depends on my walk than my talk.

D. L. Moody

$\mathcal{Y}$ou will have to make a lot of important decisions,
even though most of them may seem small at the time.
It will not be nearly so hard to make them if you remember
who you are and what your values are.

Paul C. Brownlow

It takes a long time to become young.

Pablo Picasso

Character is the sum total of a person's actions.
We cannot judge a person by the good things
he does at times; we must evaluate all the times together.
Character is attained, it is never given to us.

Oswald Chambers

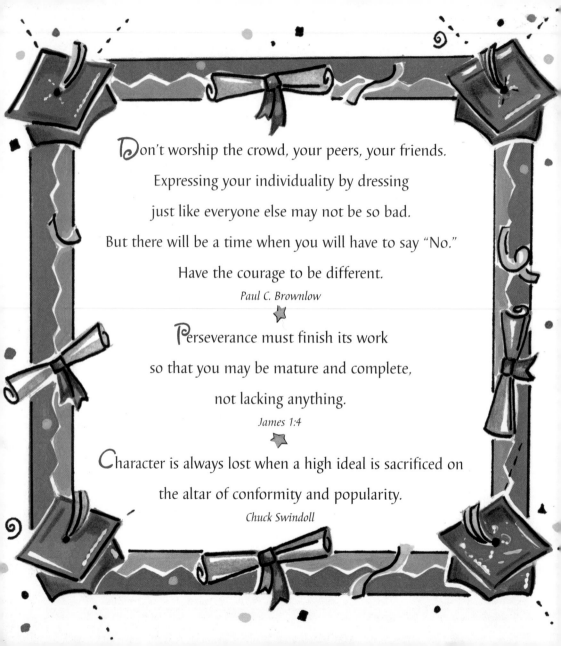

Don't worship the crowd, your peers, your friends.

Expressing your individuality by dressing

just like everyone else may not be so bad.

But there will be a time when you will have to say "No."

Have the courage to be different.

Paul C. Brownlow

Perseverance must finish its work

so that you may be mature and complete,

not lacking anything.

James 1:4

Character is always lost when a high ideal is sacrificed on

the altar of conformity and popularity.

Chuck Swindoll

There is no danger
of developing
eye strain
from looking
on the bright
side of life.

Acorns Into Oaks

Acorns don't become oak trees overnight.

The acorn starts out being small and green,

but is soon buried under a mound of dirt.

After a few fierce winters and

hot summers it becomes an oak.

It's really very simple, it just takes time!

CHAPTER THREE

Proverbs Solomon Didn't Write— But They're Still Pretty Good

Life is like an onion; you peel off

one layer at a time and sometimes you weep.

Carl Sandburg

Sometimes life is like dancing with a gorilla:

You're not done until the gorilla is.

Anonymous

To travel hopefully is a better thing than to arrive.

Robert Louis Stevenson

Happiness is a thing to be practiced, like the violin.

John Lubbock

Learn to think for yourself.

You are not everybody's dog that whistles.

Early American Proverb

All degrees of joy reside in the heart.

Oswald Chambers

The great tragedy of life is not that men perish,

but that they cease to love.

W. Somerset Maugham

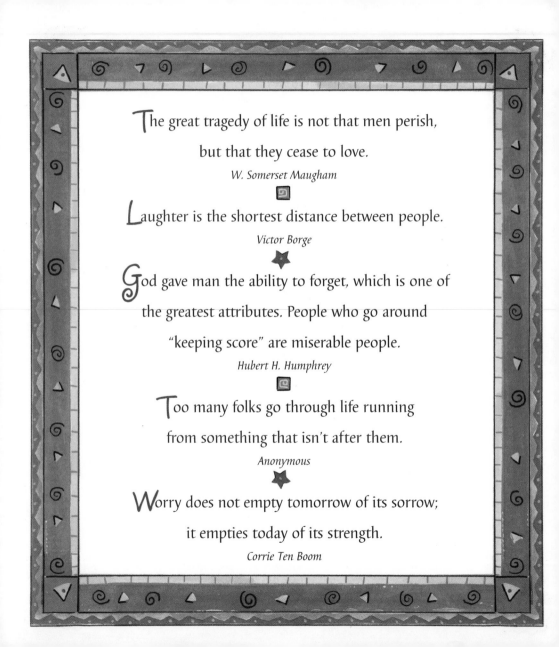

Laughter is the shortest distance between people.

Victor Borge

God gave man the ability to forget, which is one of

the greatest attributes. People who go around

"keeping score" are miserable people.

Hubert H. Humphrey

Too many folks go through life running

from something that isn't after them.

Anonymous

Worry does not empty tomorrow of its sorrow;

it empties today of its strength.

Corrie Ten Boom

*Y*esterday is history, tomorrow is a mystery,
and today is a gift; that's why they call it the present.

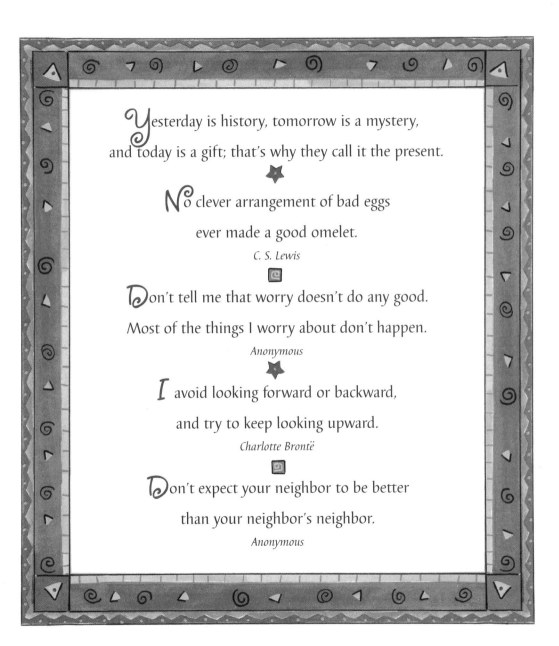

*N*o clever arrangement of bad eggs

ever made a good omelet.

C. S. Lewis

*D*on't tell me that worry doesn't do any good.

Most of the things I worry about don't happen.

Anonymous

I avoid looking forward or backward,

and try to keep looking upward.

Charlotte Brontë

*D*on't expect your neighbor to be better

than your neighbor's neighbor.

Anonymous

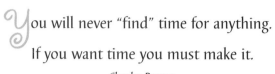
You will never "find" time for anything.

If you want time you must make it.

Charles Buxton

Our business is not to see what lies dimly at a distance,

but to do what lies clearly at hand.

Thomas Carlyle

For every minute you are angry,

you lose sixty seconds of happiness.

Anonymous

Wherever you are, be *all* there.

Charles Swindoll

Life is not so short but there is always time enough for courtesy.

Anonymous

Most of us can keep a secret. It's the people we tell it to that can't.

Anonymous

We do not love people because they are beautiful,

but they seem beautiful to us because we love them.

Russian Proverb

It is almost impossible to smile on the outside

without feeling better on the inside.

Anonymous

Love people, not things.

Use things, not people.

Paul C. Brownlow

In times like these, it helps to recall

that there have always been times like these.

Paul Harvey

CHAPTER FOUR

Family Peace and Two T.V.°s

Keeping peace in the family requires

patience, love, understanding, and at least two TV sets.

Anonymous

The family you come from isn't as important

as the family you're going to have.

Ring Lardner

Ninety percent of the friction of daily life

is caused by the wrong tone of voice.

Anonymous

Marriage is for love, for friendship, for a lifetime.

A great wedding does not make a great marriage.

Great marriages must be made and remade daily.

Paul C. Brownlow

Being married teaches us at least one very valuable lesson—

to think before we speak.

Anonymous

What right have I to make every one in the house

miserable because I am miserable? Troubles must come

to all, but troubles need not be wicked,

and it is wicked to be a destroyer of happiness.

Amelia E. Barr

Success in marriage is more than finding the right person;

it is a matter of being the right person.

Anonymous

Spare the rod and spoil the child—that is true. But,

beside the rod, keep an apple to give him when he has done well.

Martin Luther

Anyone can build a house: we need the Lord

for the creation of a home.

John Henry Jowett

Call it a clan, call it a network, call it a tribe, call it a family.

Whatever you call it, whoever you are, you need one.

Jane Howard

The Bible does not say very much about homes;

it says a great deal about the things that make them.

It speaks about life and love and joy and peace and rest!

If we get a house and put these into it,

we shall have secured a home.

John Henry Jowett

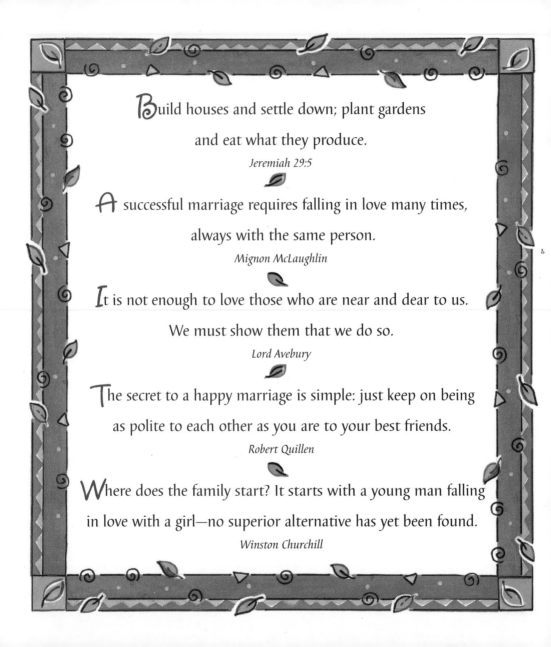

Build houses and settle down; plant gardens

and eat what they produce.

Jeremiah 29:5

A successful marriage requires falling in love many times,

always with the same person.

Mignon McLaughlin

It is not enough to love those who are near and dear to us.

We must show them that we do so.

Lord Avebury

The secret to a happy marriage is simple: just keep on being

as polite to each other as you are to your best friends.

Robert Quillen

Where does the family start? It starts with a young man falling

in love with a girl—no superior alternative has yet been found.

Winston Churchill

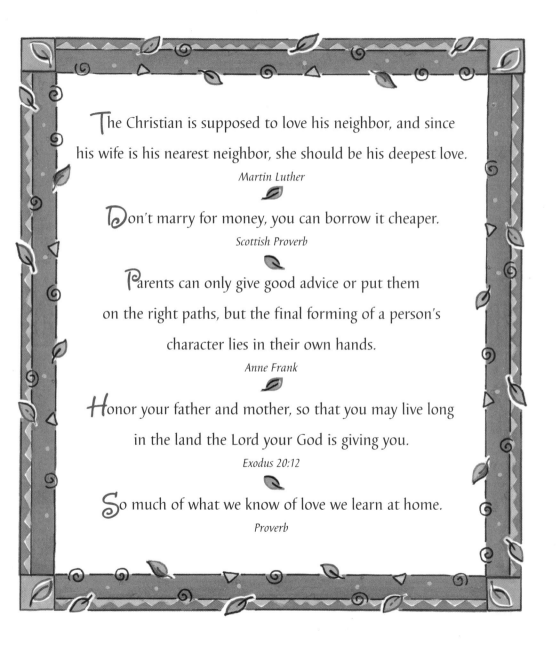

The Christian is supposed to love his neighbor, and since his wife is his nearest neighbor, she should be his deepest love.

Martin Luther

Don't marry for money, you can borrow it cheaper.

Scottish Proverb

Parents can only give good advice or put them on the right paths, but the final forming of a person's character lies in their own hands.

Anne Frank

Honor your father and mother, so that you may live long in the land the Lord your God is giving you.

Exodus 20:12

So much of what we know of love we learn at home.

Proverb

CHAPTER FIVE

No Shortcuts to Any Place Worth Going

The real voyage of discovery consists not in seeking

new landscapes, but in having new eyes.

Marcel Proust

There are no shortcuts to any place worth going.

Anonymous

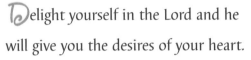

Delight yourself in the Lord and he

will give you the desires of your heart.

Psalm 37:4

I am not afraid of tomorrow for I

have seen yesterday and I love today.

William Allen White

Life has meaning,

only as one barters it day by day

for something other than itself.

Antoine de Saint Exupéry

Whatever your past, you have a spotless future.

Anonymous

The really happy
people are
the ones who
can enjoy the
scenery even when
they have to
take a detour.

Those who have a "why" to live,
can bear with almost any "how."

Victor Frankel

Therefore as God's chosen people,
holy and dearly loved, clothe yourself with compassion,
kindness, humility, gentleness and patience.

Colossians 3:12

We should all be concerned about the future because
we have to spend the rest of our lives there.

Charles Kittering

I like the dreams of the future better
than the history of the past.

Thomas Jefferson

God does not want us to do extraordinary things;
he want us to do the ordinary things extraordinarily well.

Charles Gore

Make it a rule of life never to regret

and never to look back. Regret is an

appalling waste of energy; you can't build on it.

Katherine Mansfield

Sow a thought, reap an act;

sow an act, reap a habit;

sow a habit, reap a character;

sow a character, reap a destiny.

Anonymous

CHAPTER SIX

Prayer and HOLY Chewing Gum

A prayer is not holy chewing gum and you don't

have to see how far you can stretch it.

Lionel Blue

Trust in the Lord with all your heart and lean not on your

own understanding; in all your ways acknowledge him,

and he will make your paths straight.

Proverbs 3:5

Believe in the sun, even when it does not shine.

Believe in love, even when you do not feel it.

Believe in God, even when you do not see Him.

Hans Kung (Adapted)

I am often glad that certain prayers

of my past were not granted.

C. S. Lewis

The Bible is meant to be bread for our daily use,

not just cake for special occasions.

Proverb

I used to ask God to help me.

Then I asked if I might help him.

I ended up asking him to do his work through me.

James Hudson Taylor

Dear God, help me get up; I can fall down by myself.

Anonymous

Bible study is like eating fish. When you find a bone,

you need not throw away the whole fish.

Lay aside the bone and keep eating.

Alex Wilson

It's good to spend time with God every day.

Call home and talk to your Father.

Read the letter He wrote to you.

Paul C. Brownlow

A Bible in the hand is worth two in the bookshelf.

Anonymous

An atheist is a person with no invisible means of support.

Anonymous

When men cease to wonder,

God's secrets remain unrevealed.

Anonymous

Ask, and it shall be given to you; seek,

and you will find; knock, and it shall be opened to you.

Matthew 7:7

Never make the blunder of trying to forecast the way

God is going to answer your prayer.

Oswald Chambers

CHAPTER SEVEN

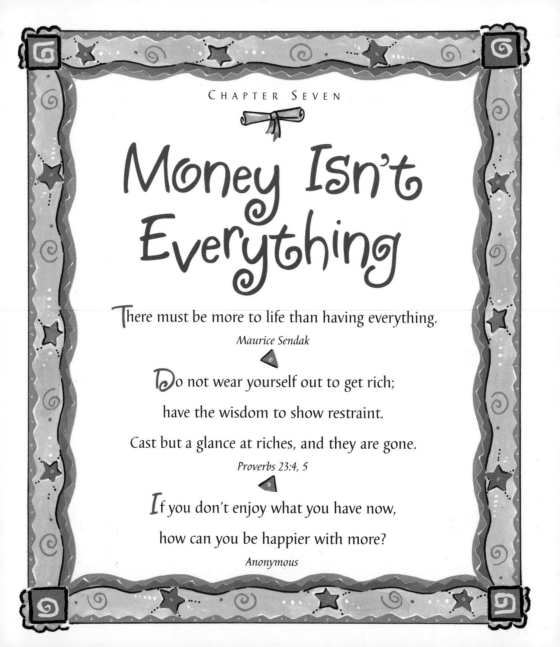

Money Isn't Everything

There must be more to life than having everything.

Maurice Sendak

Do not wear yourself out to get rich;

have the wisdom to show restraint.

Cast but a glance at riches, and they are gone.

Proverbs 23:4, 5

If you don't enjoy what you have now,

how can you be happier with more?

Anonymous

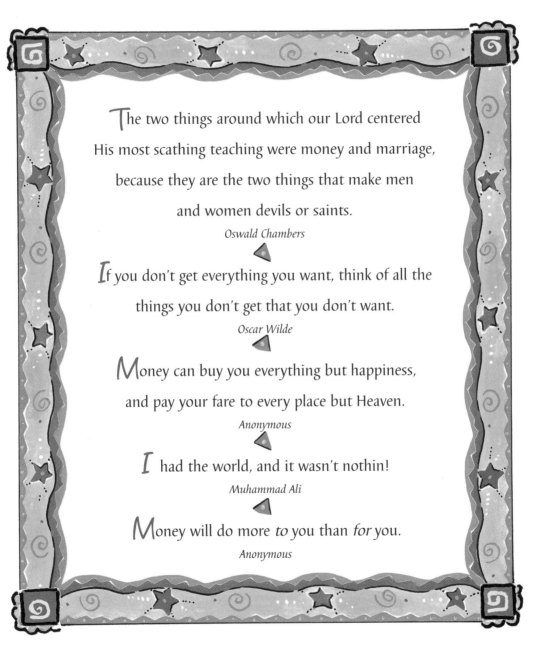

The two things around which our Lord centered
His most scathing teaching were money and marriage,
because they are the two things that make men
and women devils or saints.

Oswald Chambers

If you don't get everything you want, think of all the
things you don't get that you don't want.

Oscar Wilde

Money can buy you everything but happiness,
and pay your fare to every place but Heaven.

Anonymous

I had the world, and it wasn't nothin!

Muhammad Ali

Money will do more *to* you than *for* you.

Anonymous

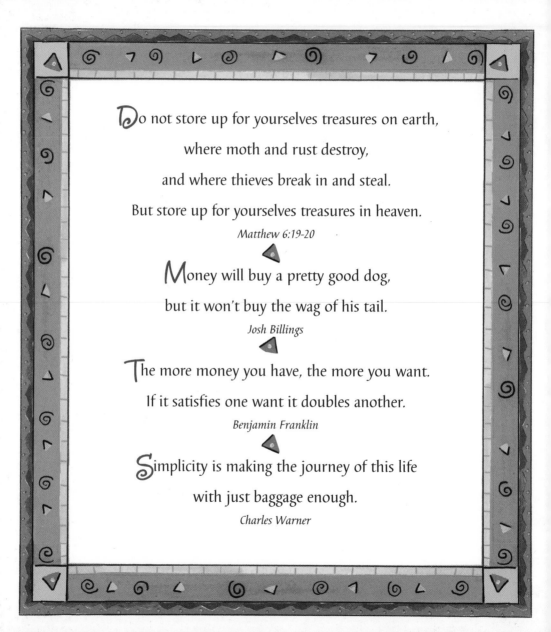

Do not store up for yourselves treasures on earth,

where moth and rust destroy,

and where thieves break in and steal.

But store up for yourselves treasures in heaven.

Matthew 6:19-20

Money will buy a pretty good dog,

but it won't buy the wag of his tail.

Josh Billings

The more money you have, the more you want.

If it satisfies one want it doubles another.

Benjamin Franklin

Simplicity is making the journey of this life

with just baggage enough.

Charles Warner

There was a time when a fool and his money were soon parted. Now it happens to everybody.

Anonymous

CHAPTER EIGHT

Life is not Fair

Life is not fair. Anyone who tells you that

is trying to sell something.

Anonymous

The tragedy of life is not that it ends so soon,

but that we wait so long to begin it.

W. M. Lewis

No one grows old by living—

only by losing interest in living.

Marie Benton Ray

There are two things to aim at in life: first, to get what you want;

and, after that, to enjoy it. Only the wisest achieve the second.

Logan Pearsall Smith

The second half of a person's life is made up

of the habits acquired during the first half.

Fyodor Dostoyevski

Do not love sleep or you will grow poor.

Proverbs 20:13

If you have made mistakes, even serious ones,

there is always another chance for you.

What we call failure is not the falling down,

but the staying down.

Mary Pickford

University
of
Life

Life is my university,
and I hope to graduate
from it with
some distinction.

Louisa May Alcott

Be glad of life
because it gives
you the chance
to love and to
work and to
play and to look
at the stars.

Henry Van Dyke

$\mathcal{A}$ heart at peace gives life to the body.

Proverbs 14:30

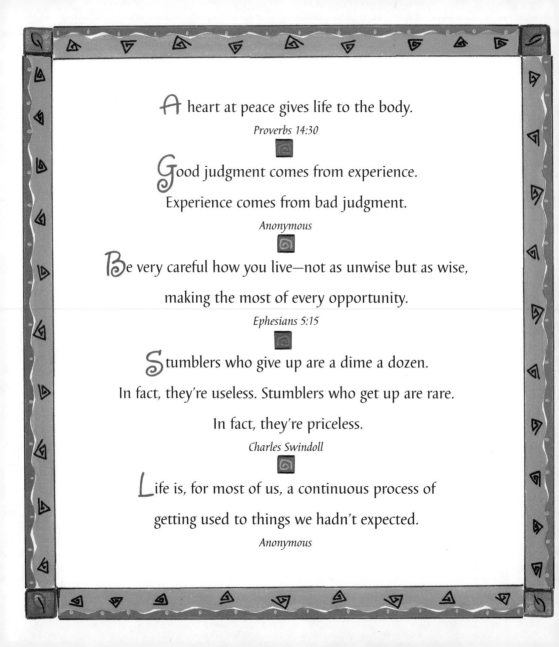

$\mathcal{G}$ood judgment comes from experience.

Experience comes from bad judgment.

Anonymous

$\mathcal{B}$e very careful how you live—not as unwise but as wise,

making the most of every opportunity.

Ephesians 5:15

$\mathcal{S}$tumblers who give up are a dime a dozen.

In fact, they're useless. Stumblers who get up are rare.

In fact, they're priceless.

Charles Swindoll

$\mathcal{L}$ife is, for most of us, a continuous process of

getting used to things we hadn't expected.

Anonymous

Try to learn from the mistakes of others.

You won't live long enough to make them all yourself.

Anonymous

Every experience God gives us,

every person he puts into our lives,

is the perfect preparation

for the future that only he can see.

Corrie Ten Boom

What lies behind us

and what lies before us are tiny matters

compared to what lies within us.

Ralph Waldo Emerson

The most important things in life are not things.

Anonymous

CHAPTER NINE

Stick With Love

I have decided to stick with love.

Hate is too great a burden to bear.

Martin Luther King, Jr.

*A*s we practice the work of forgiveness,

we discover more and more that forgiveness

and healing are one.

Agnes Sanford

*Y*our love has given me great joy.

Philemon 7

Power can do everything but the most important thing;

it cannot control love.

Philip Yancey

There is only one happiness in life, to love and be loved.

George Sand

Any time that is not spent on love is wasted.

Goethe

When you love someone, you love the whole person,

just as he or she is, and not as you would like them to be.

Leo Tolstoy

There are more people who wish to be loved

than there are willing to love.

S. R. N. Chamfort

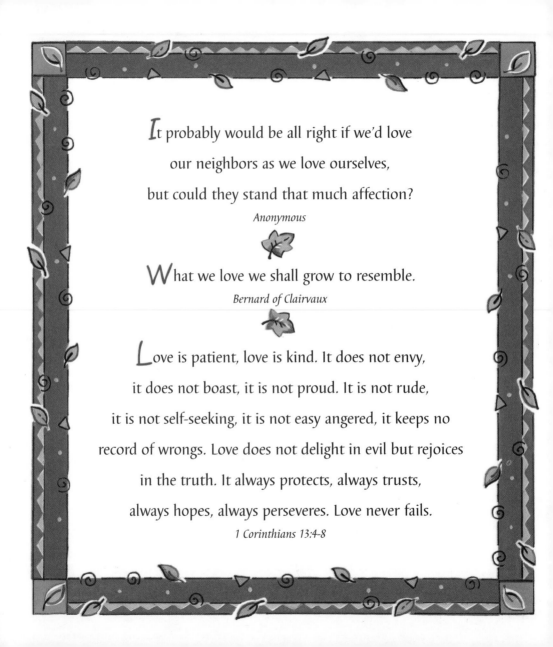

*I*t probably would be all right if we'd love

our neighbors as we love ourselves,

but could they stand that much affection?

Anonymous

*W*hat we love we shall grow to resemble.

Bernard of Clairvaux

*L*ove is patient, love is kind. It does not envy,

it does not boast, it is not proud. It is not rude,

it is not self-seeking, it is not easy angered, it keeps no

record of wrongs. Love does not delight in evil but rejoices

in the truth. It always protects, always trusts,

always hopes, always perseveres. Love never fails.

1 Corinthians 13:4-8

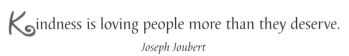

Kindness is loving people more than they deserve.

Joseph Joubert

There is a big difference between putting

your nose in other people's business and

putting your heart in other people's problems.

Anonymous

Do not waste time bothering whether you love your

neighbor; act as if you do. As soon as we do this we find one

of the great secrets. When you are behaving as

if you loved someone, you will presently come to love him.

If you injure someone you dislike, you will find yourself

disliking him more. If you do him a good turn, you will find

yourself disliking him less.

C. S. Lewis

CHAPTER TEN

Givers and Takers

We make a living by what we get,

but we make a life by what we give.

Norman MacEwan

We never live so intensely as when we

love strongly. We never realize ourselves

so vividly as when we are

in the full glow of love for others.

Walter Racschenbusch

When we forget ourselves, we usually do something

that everyone else remembers.

Anonymous

If you have love in your heart, you will always

have something to give.

Anonymous

You can give without loving,
but you cannot love without giving.

Amy Carmichael

If anyone wants to be first, he must be the very last,

and the servant of all.

Mark 9:35

Those who bring sunshine to the lives of others cannot keep it from themselves.

James M. Barrie

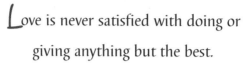

Love is never satisfied with doing or

giving anything but the best.

J. M. Gibbon

The longer I live the more I am convinced that the one thing

worth living for and dying for is the privilege of

making someone more happy and more useful. No man who

ever does anything to lift his fellows ever makes a sacrifice.

Booker T. Washington

The fragrance of what you give away stays with you.

Earl Allen

Love is not getting, but giving. It is sacrifice.

And sacrifice is glorious.

Joana Field

The only people with whom you should try to get even
are those who have helped you.

Mae Maloo

It is not what we take up, but what we give up,

that makes us rich.

Henry Ward Beecher

Goodness is something so simple:
always live for others, never to seek one's advantage.

Dag Hammarskjold

Serve one another in love.

Galatians 5:13

One makes ones own happiness

only by taking care of the happiness of others.

Bernardin de Saint-Pierre

CHAPTER ELEVEN

A Little Bit of Good Advice

Never lend people money;

it gives them amnesia.

Soupy Sales

If you will humble yourselves

under the mighty hand of God,

in his good time he will lift you up.

1 Peter 5:6

*B*e yourself. Who else is better qualified?

Frank J. Giblin II

*D*on't refuse to go on an occasional wild-goose chase;

that is what wild geese are made for.

Henry S. Haskins

*D*on't be so quick to always choose the new.

Not everything old is bad, nor everything new good.

Paul C. Brownlow

*E*ven in the common affairs of life, in love,

friendship, and marriage, how little security we have

when we trust our happiness in the hands of others!

William Hazlitt

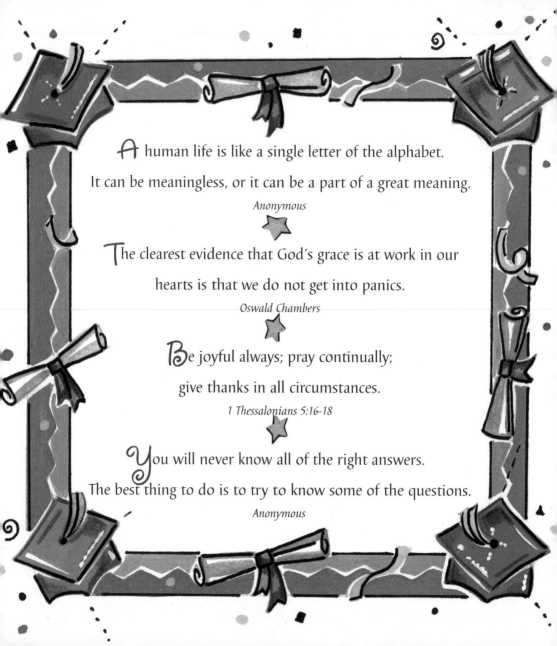

A human life is like a single letter of the alphabet.
It can be meaningless, or it can be a part of a great meaning.

Anonymous

The clearest evidence that God's grace is at work in our

hearts is that we do not get into panics.

Oswald Chambers

Be joyful always; pray continually;

give thanks in all circumstances.

1 Thessalonians 5:16-18

You will never know all of the right answers.
The best thing to do is to try to know some of the questions.

Anonymous

Make one person happy each day and in forty years
you have made 14,600 human beings happy
for a little time at least.

Anonymous

Don't sell people short. You can always find someone
ready to carry the stool when there's a piano to be moved.

Anonymous

There is a difference between being "plain" or
being a "classic." Vanilla still outsells all the other flavors.

Paul C. Brownlow

To avoid old age, keep taking on new thoughts
and throwing off old habits.

Anonymous

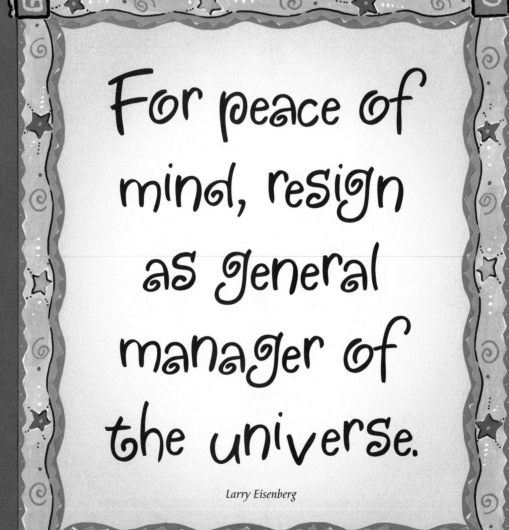

For peace of mind, resign as general manager of the universe.

Larry Eisenberg

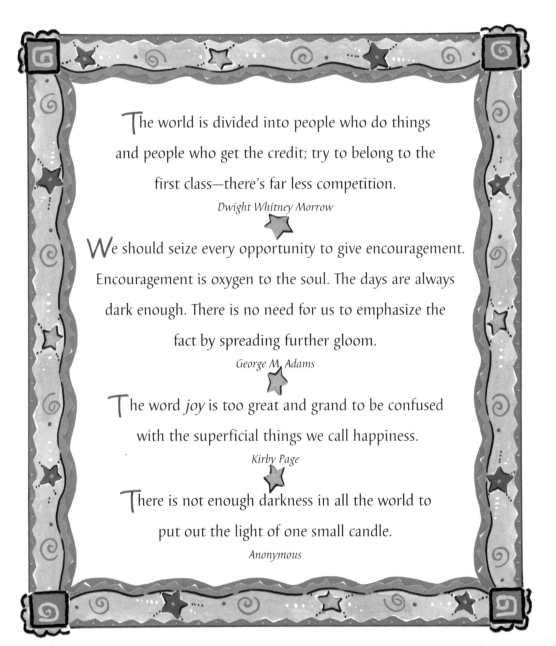

The world is divided into people who do things
and people who get the credit; try to belong to the
first class—there's far less competition.

Dwight Whitney Morrow

We should seize every opportunity to give encouragement.
Encouragement is oxygen to the soul. The days are always
dark enough. There is no need for us to emphasize the
fact by spreading further gloom.

George M. Adams

The word *joy* is too great and grand to be confused
with the superficial things we call happiness.

Kirby Page

There is not enough darkness in all the world to
put out the light of one small candle.

Anonymous

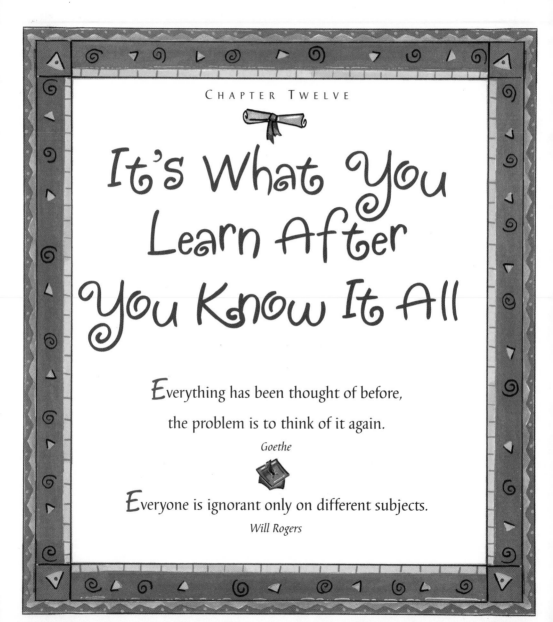

CHAPTER TWELVE

It's What You Learn After You Know It All

*E*verything has been thought of before,

the problem is to think of it again.

Goethe

*E*veryone is ignorant only on different subjects.

Will Rogers

The trouble with the world is not that people know so little,

but that they know so many things that ain't so.

Mark Twain

The Golden Rule is still true and still works:

Do unto others as you would have them do unto you.

Matthew 7:12

Never mistake knowledge for wisdom.

One helps you make a living; the other helps you make a life.

Sandra Carey

God has never turned away the questions

of a sincere searcher.

Max Lucado

One can easily recognize a wise person

by the things he does not say.

Anonymous

It's what you learn after you know

it all that really matters.

Proverb

A good listener is not only popular everywhere,

but after awhile he knows something.

Wilson Mizner

You cannot teach a man anything;

you can only help him to find it for himself.

Galileo

For the Lord grants wisdom! His every word is a treasure

of knowledge and understanding.

Proverbs 2:6

Colleges are great reservoirs of knowledge. The freshmen bring in a little every year and the seniors never take any away. And that stuff just naturally accumulates.

Abbott's Journal

Knowledge is horizontal. Wisdom is vertical—

it comes down from above.

Billy Graham

We must not expect simple answers to far-reaching

questions. However far our gaze penetrates,

there are always heights which block our vision.

Alfred North Whitehead

The whole wisdom of God has come down to the shores

of our lives in a flesh and blood Man, and John says,

we have seen Him and we know Him.

Oswald Chambers

There will never be another now—I'll make the most of today.

There will never be another me—I'll make the most of myself.

Anonymous

No one is wise all the time.

Ancient Proverb

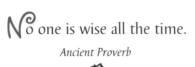

A person doesn't begin to attain wisdom until

he recognizes that he is no longer indispensible.

Admiral Richard E. Byrd

Blessed is the man who finds wisdom,

the man who gains understanding,

for she is more profitable than silver and

yields better returns than gold.

Proverbs 3:13, 14

The wise learn from tragedy;

the foolish merely repeat it.

Michael Novak

CHAPTER THIRTEEN

Enjoy the Sunshine

Some people are making such thorough preparations for a rainy day that they aren't enjoying today's sunshine.

There is a big difference between living and just breathing. Choose to live, not just exist. Use your gifts and your days wisely, deliberately. You were put here for a purpose.

Paul C. Brownlow

For the Lord God is a sun and a shield;

the Lord bestows favor and honor; no good thing does

he withhold from those whose walk is blameless.

Psalm 84:11

It is a funny thing about life. If you refuse to accept anything

but the best, you very often get it.

Somerset Maugham

I will not just live my life. I will not just spend my life.

I will invest my life.

Helen Keller

How wonderful it is that nobody need wait a single

moment before starting to improve the world.

Anne Frank

Be a life long or short, its completeness depends

on what it was lived for.

David Starr Jordan

I asked God for all things so I could enjoy life.

He gave me life so I could enjoy all things.

Anonymous

The worst bankrupt person in the world is the one

who has lost his enthusiasm.

H. W. Arnold

Fear not that your life shall come to an end,

but rather fear that it shall never have a beginning.

J. H. Newman

There is nothing new under the sun.

Ecclesiastes 1:9

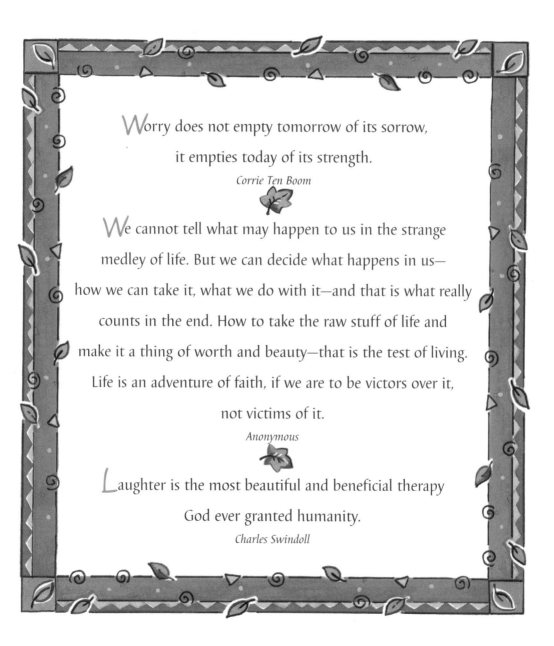

Worry does not empty tomorrow of its sorrow,

it empties today of its strength.

Corrie Ten Boom

We cannot tell what may happen to us in the strange

medley of life. But we can decide what happens in us—

how we can take it, what we do with it—and that is what really

counts in the end. How to take the raw stuff of life and

make it a thing of worth and beauty—that is the test of living.

Life is an adventure of faith, if we are to be victors over it,

not victims of it.

Anonymous

Laughter is the most beautiful and beneficial therapy

God ever granted humanity.

Charles Swindoll

God's promises are like stars; the darker the night the brighter they shine.

David Nicholas

CHAPTER FOURTEEN

God is Nuts About Us

God loves us the way we are,

but He loves us too much to leave us that way.

Leighton Ford

Love the Lord your God with all your heart

and with all your soul and with all your strength.

Deuteronomy 6:5

Our love for God is best tested by the question

of whether we seek him or his gifts.

Ralph Sockman

$\mathcal{G}$od doesn't care so much about being analyzed.

Mainly, he wants to be loved.

Philip Yancey

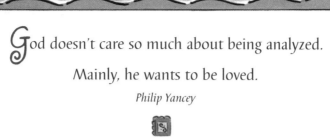

Life's greatest tragedy is to lose God and not to miss Him.

F.W. Norwood

$\mathcal{G}$od wants spiritual fruit, not religious nuts.

Anonymous

$\mathcal{A}$ttempt something so impossible that unless God is in it,

it is doomed to failure.

John Haggai

$\mathcal{Y}$ou will seek me and find me when you seek me

with all your heart. I will be found by you.

Jeremiah 29:13

We all live by faith of some kind, the non-believer
as well as the saint; the one by faith in natural law
and the other by faith in God.

A. W. Tozer

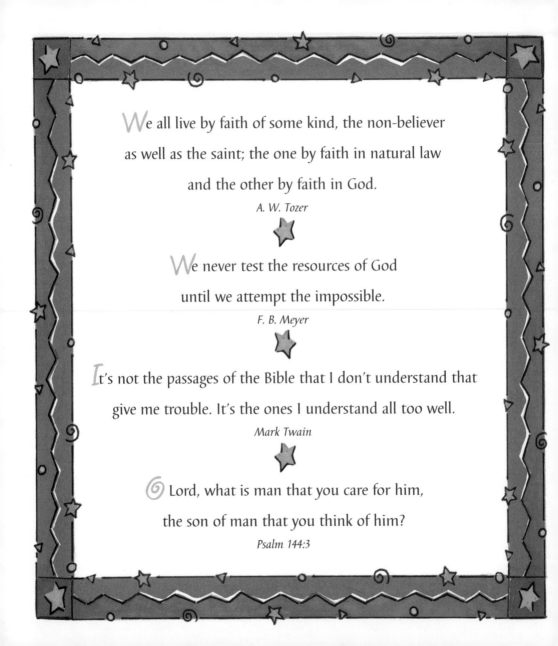

We never test the resources of God
until we attempt the impossible.

F. B. Meyer

It's not the passages of the Bible that I don't understand that
give me trouble. It's the ones I understand all too well.

Mark Twain

O Lord, what is man that you care for him,
the son of man that you think of him?

Psalm 144:3

God is nuts about us!

Rick Atchley

I've read the last page of the Bible.

It's all going to turn out all right.

Billy Graham

I can see how it might be possible for a man

to look down upon the earth and be an atheist,

but I cannot conceive how he could look up

into the heavens and say there is no God.

Abraham Lincoln

We are not human beings trying to be spiritual.

We are spiritual beings trying to be human.

Jacquelyn Small

When you know that God loves you, it helps you love yourself. And when you love yourself, you can love somebody else.

Karl Milton

God loves; not because we are lovable
but because He is love, not because He needs to receive
but because He delights to give.

C. S. Lewis

God always gives his very best to those who
leave the choice to him.

James Hudson Taylor

Without God, we cannot.

Without us, God will not.

Saint Augustine of Hippo

God still speaks to those who take the time to listen.

Anonymous

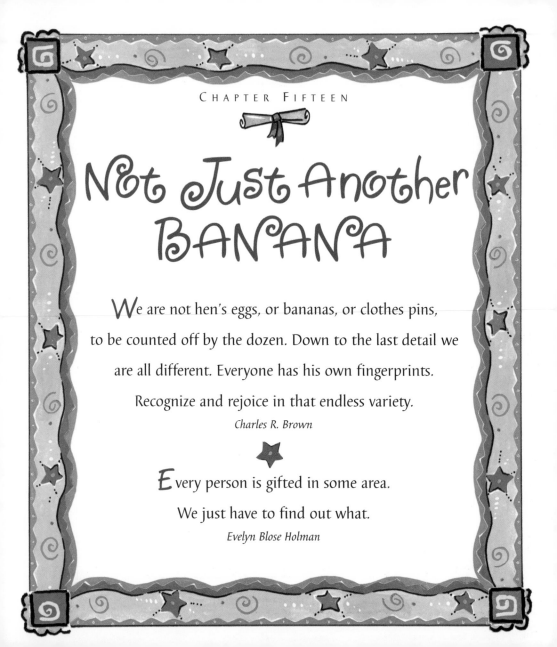

CHAPTER FIFTEEN

Not Just Another BANANA

We are not hen's eggs, or bananas, or clothes pins,
to be counted off by the dozen. Down to the last detail we
are all different. Everyone has his own fingerprints.
Recognize and rejoice in that endless variety.

Charles R. Brown

*E*very person is gifted in some area.

We just have to find out what.

Evelyn Blose Holman

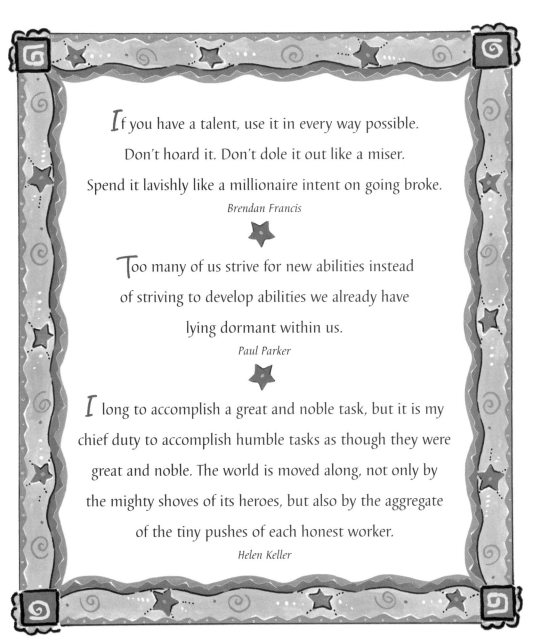

*I*f you have a talent, use it in every way possible.

Don't hoard it. Don't dole it out like a miser.

Spend it lavishly like a millionaire intent on going broke.

Brendan Francis

*T*oo many of us strive for new abilities instead

of striving to develop abilities we already have

lying dormant within us.

Paul Parker

I long to accomplish a great and noble task, but it is my

chief duty to accomplish humble tasks as though they were

great and noble. The world is moved along, not only by

the mighty shoves of its heroes, but also by the aggregate

of the tiny pushes of each honest worker.

Helen Keller

Neglect not the gift within you.

1Timothy 4:14

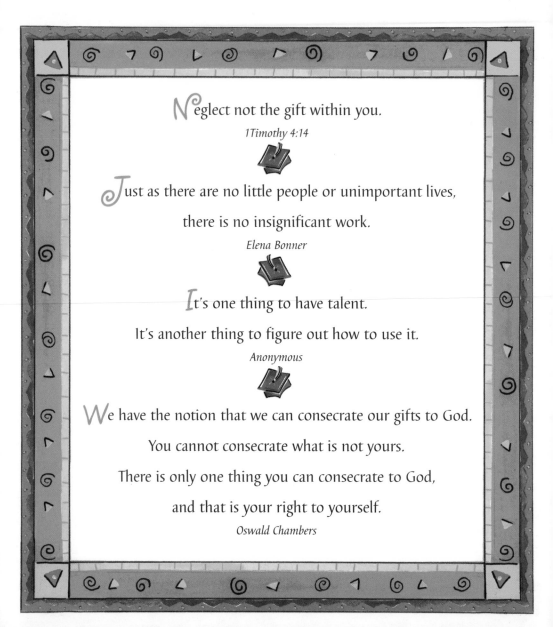

Just as there are no little people or unimportant lives,

there is no insignificant work.

Elena Bonner

It's one thing to have talent.

It's another thing to figure out how to use it.

Anonymous

We have the notion that we can consecrate our gifts to God.

You cannot consecrate what is not yours.

There is only one thing you can consecrate to God,

and that is your right to yourself.

Oswald Chambers

Don't envy anybody. We all have something no one else has.

Develop that one thing and make it outstanding.

Anonymous

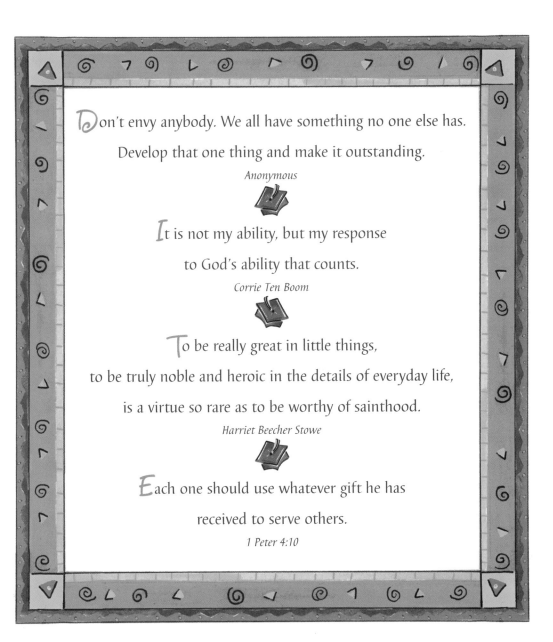

It is not my ability, but my response

to God's ability that counts.

Corrie Ten Boom

To be really great in little things,

to be truly noble and heroic in the details of everyday life,

is a virtue so rare as to be worthy of sainthood.

Harriet Beecher Stowe

Each one should use whatever gift he has

received to serve others.

1 Peter 4:10

CHAPTER SIXTEEN

Becoming an Overnight Success

*I*t usually takes 20 years

to become an overnight success.

Eddie Cantor

I have learned that success is to be measured

not so much by the position that one has reached

in life as by the obstacles which he has overcome

while trying to succeed.

Booker T. Washington

I'd rather be a failure at something I enjoy,

than be a success at something I hate.

George Burns

*B*eware of succumbing to failure as inevitable;

make it the stepping-stone to success.

Oswald Chambers

*I*f a person wakes up famous,

he hasn't been sleeping.

Wes Izzard

*S*omebody is always doing what

somebody else said couldn't be done.

Anonymous

The closer one gets to the top, the more one finds there is no "top."

Nancy Barcus

ALISON

You talk to yourself all the time,

be careful what you say.

Negative thoughts are destructive.

William Lantz

The two hardest things to handle in life

are failure and success.

Anonymous

God has not called me to be successful;

he has called me to be faithful.

Mother Teresa

Commit to the Lord whatever you do,

and your plans will succeed.

Proverbs 16:3

He has achieved success who has lived well,

laughed often, and loved much.

Bessie Anderson Stanley

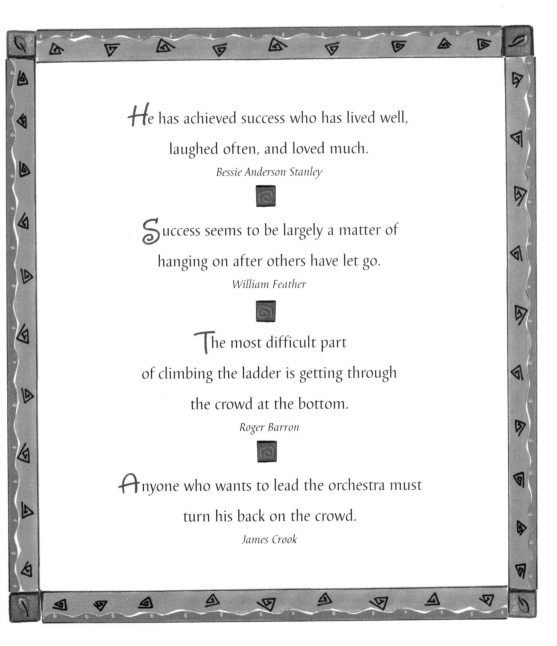

Success seems to be largely a matter of

hanging on after others have let go.

William Feather

The most difficult part

of climbing the ladder is getting through

the crowd at the bottom.

Roger Barron

Anyone who wants to lead the orchestra must

turn his back on the crowd.

James Crook

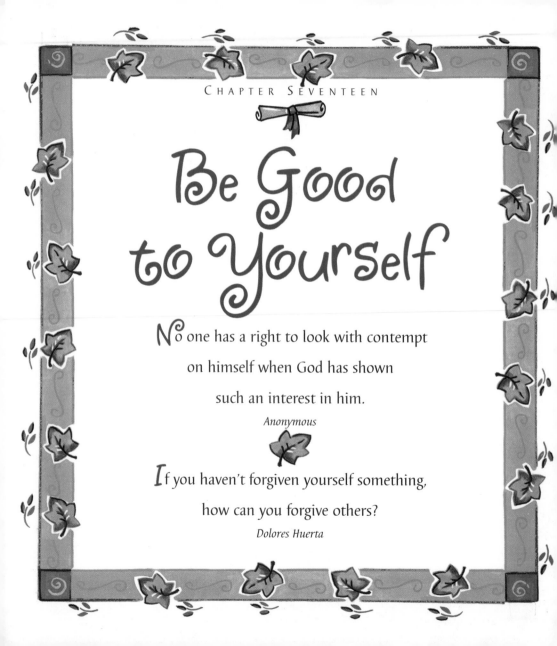

CHAPTER SEVENTEEN

Be Good to Yourself

No one has a right to look with contempt

on himself when God has shown

such an interest in him.

Anonymous

If you haven't forgiven yourself something,

how can you forgive others?

Dolores Huerta

My Dad always told me to "be good to yourself."

It's taken a long time, but I think

I finally know what he meant.

Paul C. Brownlow

The world is full of cactus,

but we don't have to sit on it.

Anonymous

No one can make you feel inferior without your consent.

Eleanor Roosevelt

Love your neighbor as yourself.

Leviticus 19:18

Think well of yourself.

The world takes you at your own estimate.

Alfred Montapert

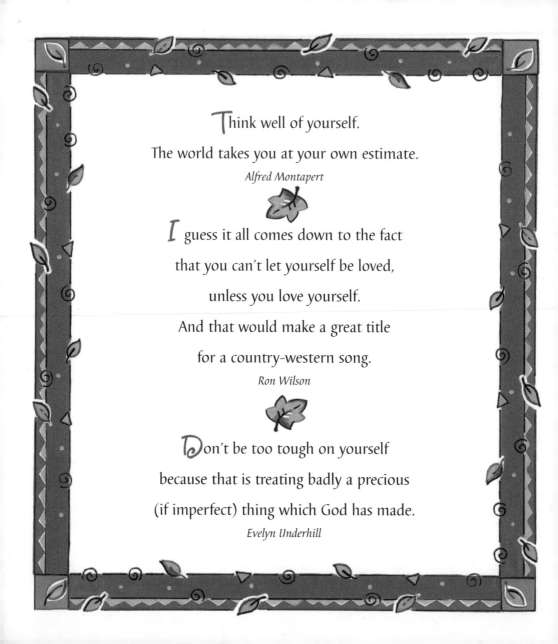

I guess it all comes down to the fact

that you can't let yourself be loved,

unless you love yourself.

And that would make a great title

for a country-western song.

Ron Wilson

Don't be too tough on yourself

because that is treating badly a precious

(if imperfect) thing which God has made.

Evelyn Underhill